COUNTRY

AUSTRALIA

COUNTRY
AUSTRALIA

NICK RAINS

EXPLORE
AUSTRALIA

CONTENTS

FOREWORD

Many of us harbour a dream of escaping to the country. Whether it be a temporary respite from the pressure cooker of urban life, or to serve a more fundamental need for a deeper connection to the land and the perceived simplicity of a life lived in tune with the cycles and seasons of nature, it's a common enough yearning among the 70 per cent of Australians who inhabit our big cities.

The sight that's guaranteed to make my own heart skip a beat is the end of the bitumen and the start of an unsealed road. For me, it signals the beginning of the next adventure and the promise of a road less travelled – better still if that road stretches ahead empty, all the way to the shimmering horizon, under an expansive, impossibly blue sky.

It was out there, under those big and often unforgiving skies, that the modern nation of Australia was forged, and we still like to define our national character with the pioneering values of grit, resourcefulness, larrikinism and a certain disregard for pen-pushing authority. The early European settlers entered into a pitched battle with this ancient island continent. There were victories and losses, and any journey, east to west or north to south, will reveal the symbols of both: orchards, vineyards and furrowed fields; vast plains dotted with sheep; cattle runs on the scale of some small sovereign nations. These visions testify to a successful taming of the land, while at the margins stand derelict stone cottages and abandoned windmills – silent epitaphs to lost struggles and the fickle nature of the weather, the climate and commodity prices.

And then there are the truly wild places that have continued to thwart all attempts at subjugation and remain productive only to Australia's original human inhabitants. Australia's blessed with wilderness, substantial tracts of which lie within cooee of our biggest cities. But the real magic is the reward of a long journey that ends with an immersion in a truly remote and monumental landscape.

These visions of sky and stone are a continual source of inspiration for artists of all disciplines, and none more so than photographer Nick Rains. Like me, Nick originally hails from the industrial north of England. The contrast is obvious, and the effect has been profound. A drive to capture and communicate the beauty and the wonder has led Nick on many adventures across his adopted homeland in pursuit of his craft. This book serves to showcase his gift for framing his vision in the perfect light, with an eye for both the big picture and the revealing detail. The romance of rural life is expertly expressed, alongside the allure of the landforms and the unique nature of our native fauna and flora.

Chrissie Goldrick
Editor-in-Chief, *Australian Geographic*

INTRODUCTION

Even though the vast majority of Australians live within 50 kilometres of the coast, as a nation we still identify with the inland areas of the continent – the outback, country Australia, call it what you will. It's in our national character: even the most urbane city dweller, deep down, has a hankering to 'go bush' at some point, to see what the country really looks like and to experience the vastness of the inland realm.

This book encompasses a huge variety of places in inland Australia – pretty much anywhere that is not the coast or a city! There are images from the deep outback, where you need a four-wheel-drive vehicle to visit safely, through to the thriving agricultural communities of the coastal hinterland. I have made no attempt to be geographically comprehensive in my coverage; the locations featured in this book are simply places that I have enjoyed visiting over the past 25 years, places that have resonated with me both as a photographer and as a visitor.

I have been most fortunate in my career to be able to spend a lot of time on the road, travelling lesser known routes and following my nose down interesting side tracks that take my fancy. I have stumbled across amazing locations entirely by accident, I have been given good advice by locals and I have, on rare occasions, been led totally up the garden path, to places I'd rather forget!

Having said that, nowhere I've been was ever a total waste of time. Good photographs can be taken anywhere, even if they're not necessarily the ones you set out to take in the first place. If I have learned anything as a documentary photographer, it's to be open to opportunities and not be locked into preconceived ideas about how a place should look.

With so many people taking photographs these days, it's often said that it's hard to find new places to photograph and that it's all been done before. While this is true to a certain extent, everyone has their own way of seeing, and you can put a group of photographers into a situation at the same place on the same day and they will all come up with different images. I once worked with a group of five talented photographers travelling together and, yes, we came away with very different interpretations of the same places.

I get to meet an amazing variety of people on my travels. The population of the outback may be only a fraction of the total number of Australians, but, as a group, country folk punch well above their weight in terms of character! On a recent assignment for the South Australian Government, I was tasked with shooting images on the theme of 'community'. This meant concentrating not on the 'where' but on the 'who'. Looking back, it was one of my most satisfying journeys ever. I photographed outback golf in 40°C-plus heat, local fund-raising events, opal miners, wheat farmers, school concert practices, outback pubs and more. Together these shoots involved a huge range of people in many different locations. Without exception, everyone I met could not have been more friendly and helpful.

Even after many years of travelling the back roads of this big continent, I still relish the opportunity to head off once more. I know it sounds clichéd, but the lure of the open road is still there. I love the fact that you can turn a corner and find a totally new image. Or, equally satisfying, go back to a familiar place and see something you've never seen before.

Nick Rains

The setting sun highlights dust thrown up by cattle, at Home Valley Station in the Kimberley, Western Australia.

DRY

ANY continent will have a wide range of climate types. Australia can be very cold and wet, or baking hot and dry, or any combination thereof. But of all these categories, dry is probably the one that springs to mind first when people talk about Australia – and with good cause.

There are parts of the country where, during particularly arid spells, it might not rain for years. And even during 'normal' weather, central regions may not see a drop of water for the entire dry season. As a result of these extremes of climate, the landforms and inhabitants are dramatically shaped, both in obvious and not-so-obvious ways.

Flying over the Simpson Desert at first light (p. 10) was a genuine treat. As a photographer, I am always looking for ways to make my images more compelling and seeing this vast area of parallel dunes from the air for the first time was exciting. From the ground you get no idea of the scale, but from 150 metres up in the air the dunes seem to recede into infinity, giving you a clear sense of how big the outback really is.

The Devils Marbles, north of Tennant Creek in the Northern Territory, often appear to glow in the fading dusk light.

Marree, in northern South Australia, preserves some of the last remnants of the former Central Australian Railway. Early morning offers cool respite before daytime temperatures soar beyond 40°C.

carving out *an* existence *in* *the* **back** *of* **beyond** *is not for* *the* *faint-hearted*

Wool-bale rolling is one of the more light-hearted events at the Blinman Gymkhana, South Australia.

Grass sprouts from the walls of Kalamina Gorge, Karijini National Park, in the Pilbara region, Western Australia.

the human **impact** on **nature** can sometimes
seem almost **insignificant**

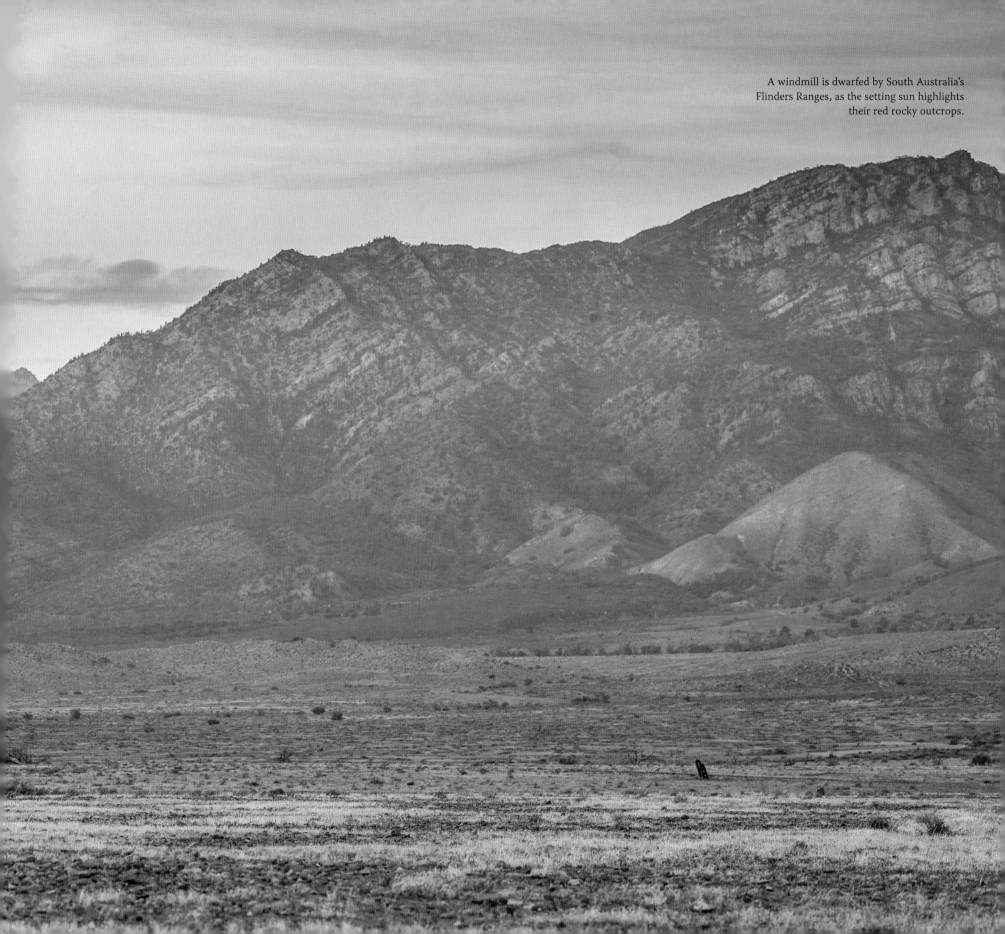

A windmill is dwarfed by South Australia's Flinders Ranges, as the setting sun highlights their red rocky outcrops.

ABOVE Morning light accentuates the serpentine shapes of the seemingly endless sand dunes of the Simpson Desert, in Cravens Peak Reserve, near Boulia, Queensland.

RIGHT Located near Sandstone, Western Australia, this spectacular rock arch, known as London Bridge, frames the view beautifully.

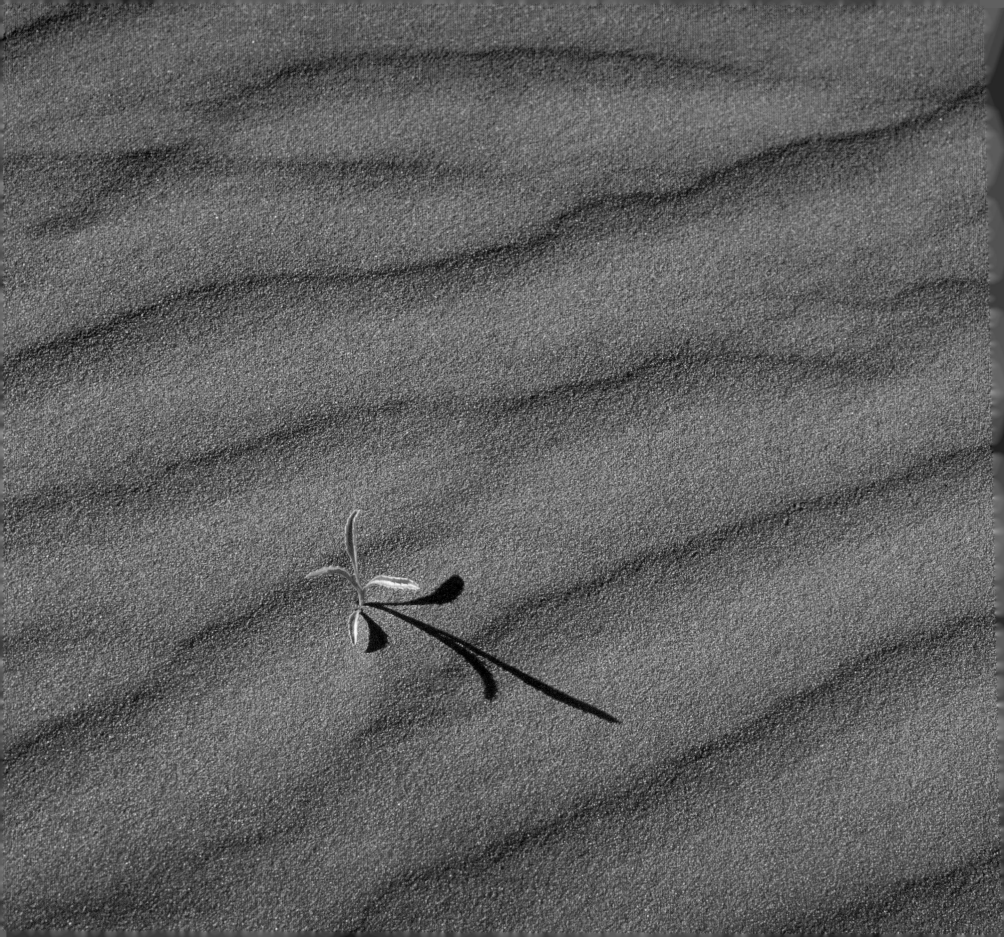

ABOVE Moonrise and a dusk 'glow' illuminate a boab at Sir John Gorge, Mornington Station, Western Australia.

LEFT Even in the driest parts of Queensland's Simpson Desert, life finds a way.

ABOVE Workers build exclusion fencing during revegetation research on Muggon Station, near Mullewa, Western Australia.

RIGHT Tufts of grass sprout after early-season fires on Mornington Station, in the Kimberley, Western Australia.

Rare clouds add texture and drama to a
dawn sky in the western Simpson Desert.

harsh, flat desert against
the sweeping curves of
the dunes – nature's contrasts

CLOCKWISE FROM TOP River red gums line a dry watercourse in Bimbowrie Conservation Park, near Olary, South Australia; a perentie (Australia's largest monitor lizard or goanna) on the hunt in Cravens Peak Reserve, near Boulia, Queensland; a scorpion raises its tail, ready to sting, in Gluepot Reserve, north of Waikerie, South Australia; emus wander through grassland near Blinman, South Australia.

the play of reflected *sunlight* reveals *the textures in the* rocks

Echidna Chasm, in Purnululu National Park, Western Australia, splits the conglomerate escarpment, narrowing to less than 2 metres wide as its walls rise 100 metres.

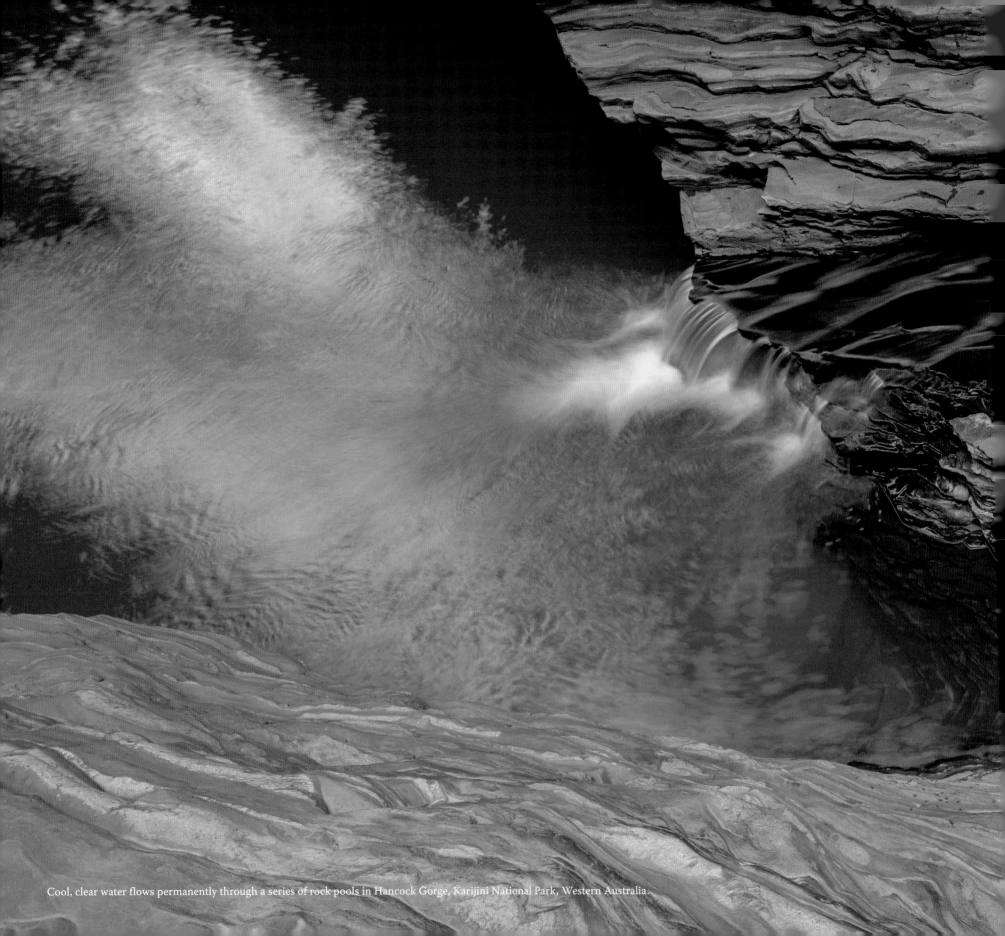

Cool, clear water flows permanently through a series of rock pools in Hancock Gorge, Karijini National Park, Western Australia.

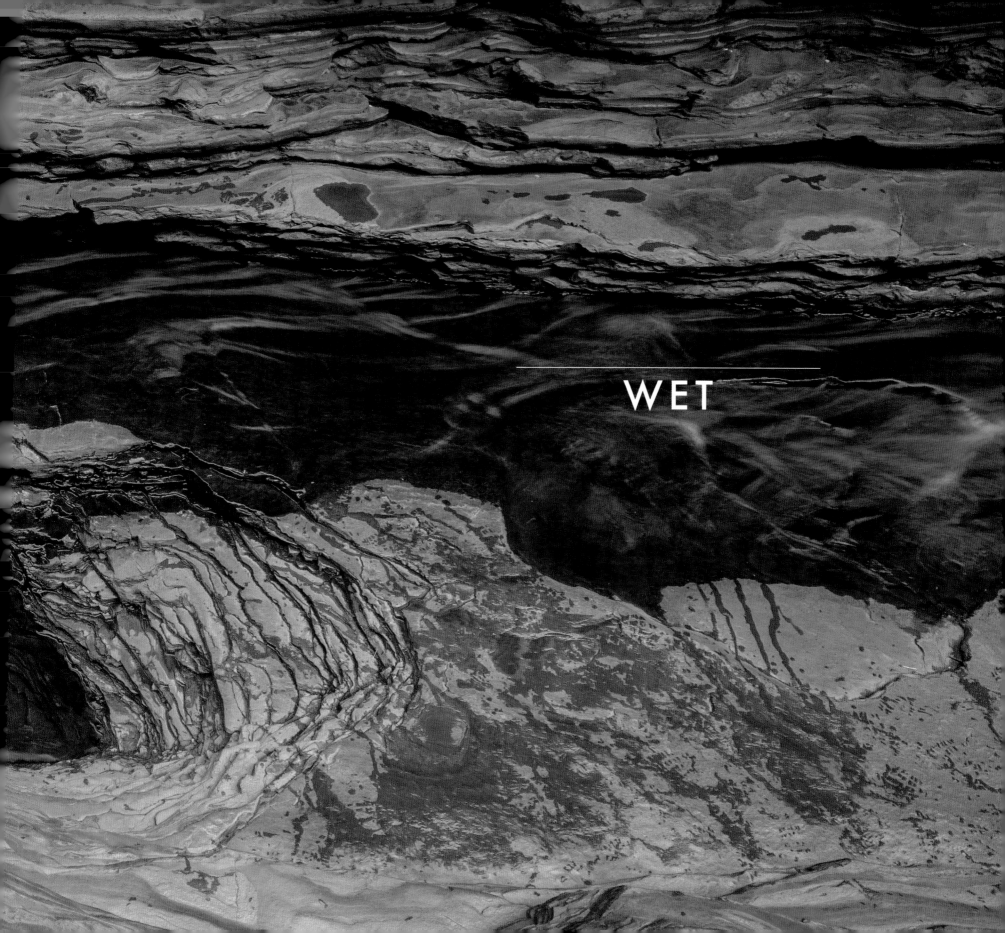

WET

LIFE needs water, and even though Australia is famous for burning-hot, arid deserts, there are many parts of the country where the opposite is true and water flows and life flourishes. The far north of Queensland has rainfall far exceeding that of most parts of Europe, and the south-eastern states have river systems that run for thousands of kilometres. Parts of the central deserts flood fairly regularly and the seemingly 'dead' centre can spring to life in a matter of days after good rains.

And even within the harshest and most arid areas, there is often permanent water. The Pilbara region is mostly known for its huge iron-ore mines and the deep red of its earth, but within the gorges of Karijini National Park permanent springs keep the pools full year-round and even on the hottest days they remain icy cold. Hancock Gorge (pp. 22, 32 and 40) is one of the more difficult locations to access in Karijini – you have to swim through one gorge to get to the deepest parts – and it's always a surprise to me just how cold that water can be!

no breeze to counter the humidity, but
a perfect mirror for the evening sky

Capturing this image of Cooper Creek
Billabong, at Mount Borradaile in the
Northern Territory, involved floating in
a tinnie and trying not to disturb
the surface of the water.

Low-lying fog drifts over Baroon Dam at dawn, in Queensland's Sunshine Coast hinterland.

Viewed from the air, the abstract shape of a shallow lagoon, near Bremer Bay, Western Australia, reflects a vivid blue sky.

Following rains, flocks of plumed whistling ducks descend on the lakes of Diamantina National Park in western Queensland.

A permanent aquifer feeds Jirndawarrunha (Chinderwarriner) Pool, in Millstream–Chichester National Park, Western Australia.

A cruise boat makes an early start on Yellow Water Billabong, in Kakadu National Park, Northern Territory.

engine shut down, drifting silently
through the dawn mist, searching for crocs

ABOVE Northern Rockhole, reached via the Jatbula Trail, in Nitmiluk National Park is one of the lesser known sites around Katherine, in the Northern Territory.

LEFT The cool, clear water in Hancock Gorge, Karijini National Park, Western Australia, contrasts with the adjacent red-rock ledges.

gentle reflections belie the *fierce* blizzards *whipping* over the *distant* peak

Set at the edge of Dove Lake, in Cradle Mountain–
Lake St Clair National Park, Tasmania, a 1940s
boatshed looks a little forlorn in winter.

ABOVE A saltwater crocodile 'gapes' in the early-morning sun in Kakadu National Park, Northern Territory.

RIGHT A majestic old gum overhangs a billabong at Mount Augustus, Western Australia.

Sunlit water covers the flood plains near Ubirr Rock, in Kakadu National Park, Northern Territory.

as the sun **sinks** *towards the* **horizon,**
the air **fills** *with the sounds of* **birdcalls**

Climbing through the narrow chasm of Hancock Gorge, in Karijini National Park, Western Australia, reveals a majestic rockscape.

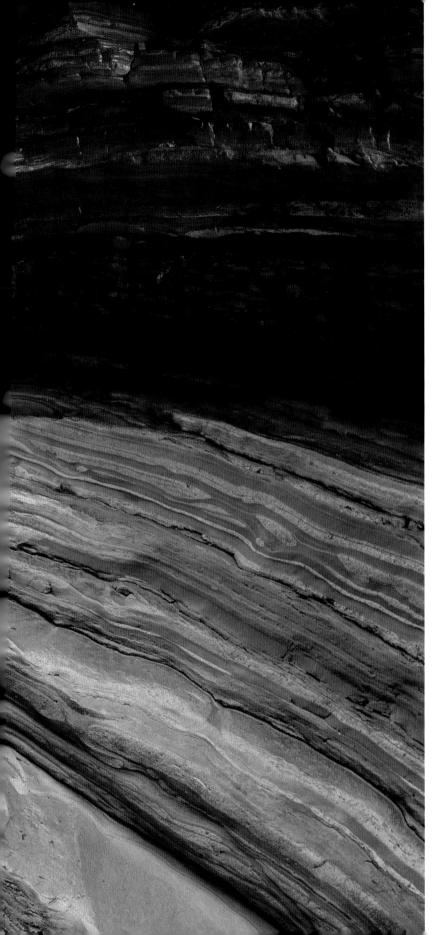

A delicate veil of water covers mossy sandstone steps at Liffey Falls, Deloraine, Tasmania.

The Taggerty River winds through the verdant Yarra Ranges in Victoria.

A cloud bursts over harvested
wheat fields, near Merriden,
Western Australia.

A lone figure perches atop Hanging Rock at dawn,
in Blue Mountains National Park, New South Wales.

BIG PICTURE

SOME of the best-known views in the world can be found right here in Australia. There are endless skies, grand vistas, a powerful sense of remoteness, even places where the silence is so complete that it makes you feel quite insignificant in the grand scheme of things. It's the land of the Big Picture.

Standing on the edge of a towering cliff and gazing out into the Grose Valley in the Blue Mountains of New South Wales gives you a sense of the scale of this immense continent. Distant ridgelines march off towards the far horizon, and you have to look hard to see signs of human impact. Hanging Rock (pp. 46–7) must be one of the most vertiginous places I have ever been to – the overhang looms over a 100 metre drop and the prow is less than 1 metre wide. If you are wondering who that idiot is in the photo, well, that would be me. I set up the shot and had a colleague press the shutter. I needed a figure for scale and it turned out I was the only one game enough to stand in the right spot.

aside from the occasional roar of a hot-air burner, we ride in complete, captivating silence

Ballooning soon after sunrise over the Byron Bay hinterland, in northern New South Wales, reveals a wonderful view to the ocean.

A colourful dawn sky forms a dramatic backdrop to Queensland's Glasshouse Mountains, viewed from Wild Horse Mountain Lookout.

Countless opium poppies
stretch as far as the eye can
see, in central Tasmania.

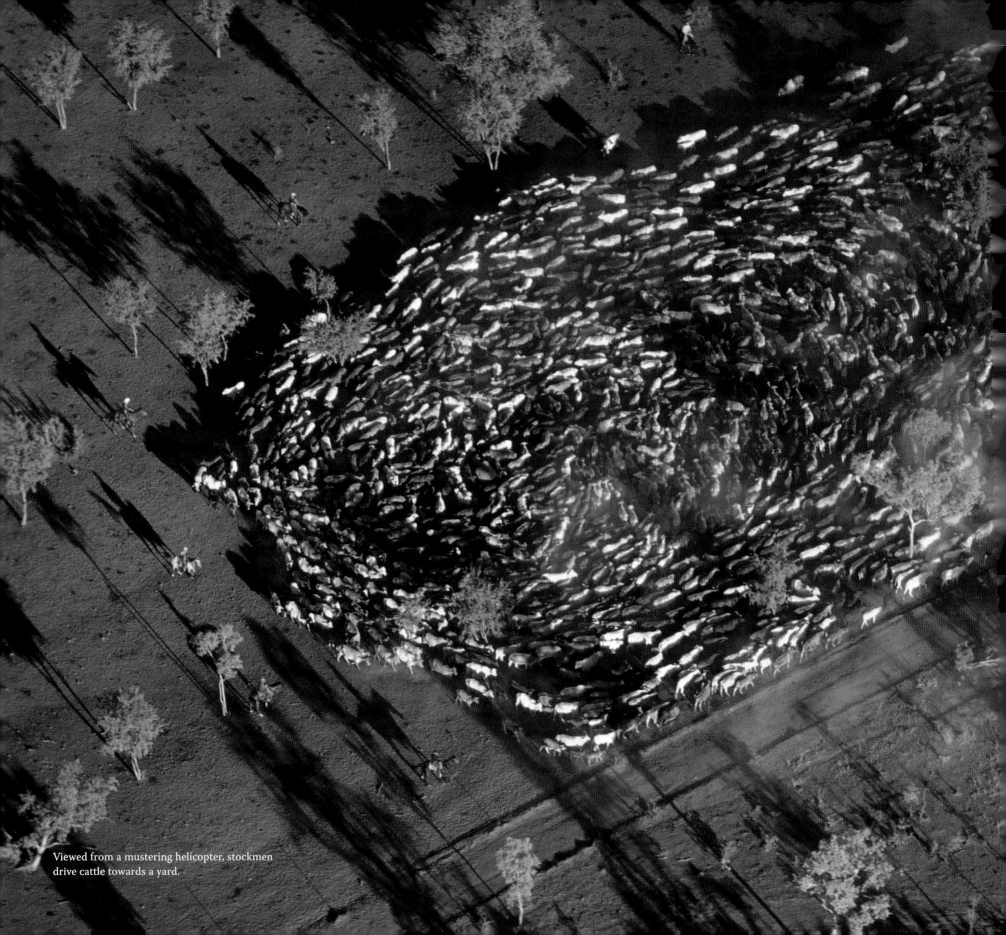

Viewed from a mustering helicopter, stockmen drive cattle towards a yard.

A haven for wildlife and a great place to cool off on a hot day, Butterfly Gorge, in the Northern Territory, is also a special site for Indigenous Australians.

The ancient caldera around
Mount Warning, in northern
New South Wales, has a
primeval look especially when
swathed in mist.

day after *day*, this *summit* is the *first* place on the **continent** to meet the *rising* sun

ABOVE A full moon rises above the Great Walls of China, near Blinman in the Flinders Ranges, South Australia.

RIGHT In Nambung National Park, near Cervantes, Western Australia, a forest of limestone formations rises from the sand.

folds of the Great *Dividing* Range
enclose *idyllic* pastures

Early-morning fog fills Condamine Gorge, near Killarney in southern Queensland.

ABOVE   The Bungle Bungles in Purnululu National Park, Western Australia, are a vast array of striped sandstone domes.

LEFT   Wilpena Pound, in South Australia's Flinders Ranges, forms a spectacular backdrop to a lone wind-driven water pump.

the *first* light of day *picks* out the *folds* of *ancient*, crumpled *rock* strata

The walls of the Elder Ranges, next to Wilpena Pound in the
Flinders Ranges, South Australia, soar to a height of 1128 metres.

The sun appears briefly during a stormy dusk at Whiskey Bay, on Wilsons Promontory, Victoria.

The last rays of the sun catch the summit of Cradle Mountain, above Dove Lake, Tasmania, on a bitterly cold day.

DETAIL

Birdlife Australia's Gluepot Reserve,
north of Waikerie, South Australia,
protects diverse wildlife, including the
western pygmy possum.

AUSTRALIA is well known for its grand, often epic scenery – in the outback, along the coast and even in the cities. Taking in these classic vistas is rewarding, but so is taking the time to examine the smaller things around you. Dew on a gum leaf on a misty morning in the Victorian Alps, the symmetry and rich colours of flowering eucalypts, and even the rusty tin walls of an outback shed can all be rewarding sights for the observant.

I try to keep my images as real as possible, but occasionally you need to set things up. The photo of the western pygmy possum (pp. 70–1) would be an almost impossible image to make in the wild because these creatures are small, shy, rare and nocturnal. My trip to Gluepot Reserve in South Australia coincided with a visit by some researchers from a university in Adelaide, and they were setting up pit trap lines to survey the local marsupial population. I was able to follow the researchers as they checked the traps early each morning and then grab images of the animals as they were released. So it's a genuine 'wild' shot, but made under controlled conditions.

Overcast skies accentuate bark patterns on the trunk of a towering gum at Dungrove Station, Lake Echo, Tasmania.

Water streams down the mossy
cliff face of Guide Falls near
Burnie, Tasmania.

CLOCKWISE FROM TOP LEFT Insects buzz among spectacular gum blossoms in the Flinders Ranges, South Australia; the moon rises behind a grove of grass trees near Bridgetown, Western Australia; vivid orange gum blossom blooms on the Jatbula Trail, Northern Territory; Sturt's desert peas dot the Pilbara landscape in Western Australia.

A twisted, stunted tree clings
to a rocky cliff face in Kalamina
Gorge, Karijini National Park,
Western Australia.

The tiniest crevice is enough for this tree to gain a roothold in the Kennedy Range, east of Carnarvon, Western Australia.

*even in **biodiversity** hot spots, **creatures** remain shy and **elusive***

A brown tree snake hangs
from a branch in a rainforest
near Murwillumbah, northern
New South Wales.

CLOCKWISE FROM RIGHT The colours of this Leichhardt grasshopper at Mount Borradaile, Northern Territory, made it easy to spot; this dainty purple-crowned fairy-wren at Mornington Station, in the Kimberley, Western Australia, has been tagged by researchers; a banded honeyeater extracts nectar from a flower on Mornington Station, Western Australia; the eastern robin creates a bright splash of colour in Lamington National Park, Queensland; late-season grapes ripen on the vine at Pemberton, Western Australia; a neat parade of Spinifex pigeons warm up after a cold night at Lorna Glen Station, near Wiluna, Western Australia.

ABOVE Washed and polished granite stones cover a beach in Noosa National Park, Queensland.

RIGHT Palm trees sprout amid boulders on Mornington Station in the Kimberley, Western Australia.

Galahs settle in to roost for the night on electricity cables,
in Cravens Peak Reserve, near Boulia, Queensland.

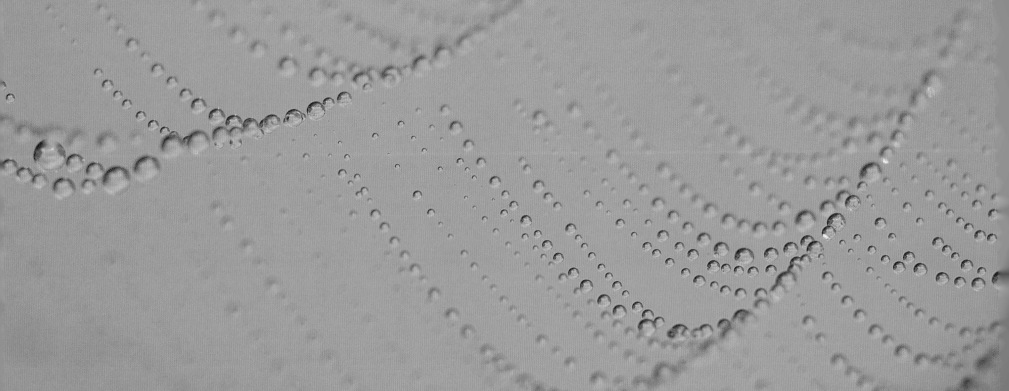

beauty can be found in **distant**, remote
realms, but also in your **backyard**

CLOCKWISE FROM LEFT Dew covers a spider web in a Brisbane eucalypt forest; a jacana balances on water plants while foraging in McCreadies Billabong, Litchfield National Park, Northern Territory; a yellow-footed rock wallaby eyes the camera warily, near Hawker, South Australia; an echidna crosses a salt pan in Bladensburg National Park, Queensland.

A saltwater crocodile lies in wait for
unsuspecting prey in Cooper Creek at
Mount Borradaile, Northern Territory.

PAST

The old woolscour at Blackall, Queensland, has been lovingly restored. The mechanisms used to clean the wool make surprisingly little noise when the power belts whir into action.

AUSTRALIA, from a white-settlement point of view, is only a tad over 200 years old, but from the perspective of the Indigenous people of the continent it's anything up to 50,000 years old.

No matter what your heritage, the past always informs and influences the present, so it's no surprise that, as a nation, we value our history and, as much as possible, try to understand where we have come from and why.

Photographers love old things – the rustier and grungier the better. I am no exception, and old shearing sheds are a favourite subject of mine. The shed at Muggon Station, at the edge of the Gibson Desert (p. 99), had a suspended floor, and at a certain time of day the low sun shone underneath, illuminating the shed interior from below. The effect only lasted a short while, so I had to make the most of the opportunity and shoot quickly.

After 150 years as a sheep run, Boolcoomatta Station, near Olary, South Australia, is now a reserve owned by Bush Heritage Australia. This is the original shearing shed.

Mist shrouds majestic Antarctic beech
trees at Springbrook, Queensland.
The trees are an ancient link to the
Gondwanan forests of the past.

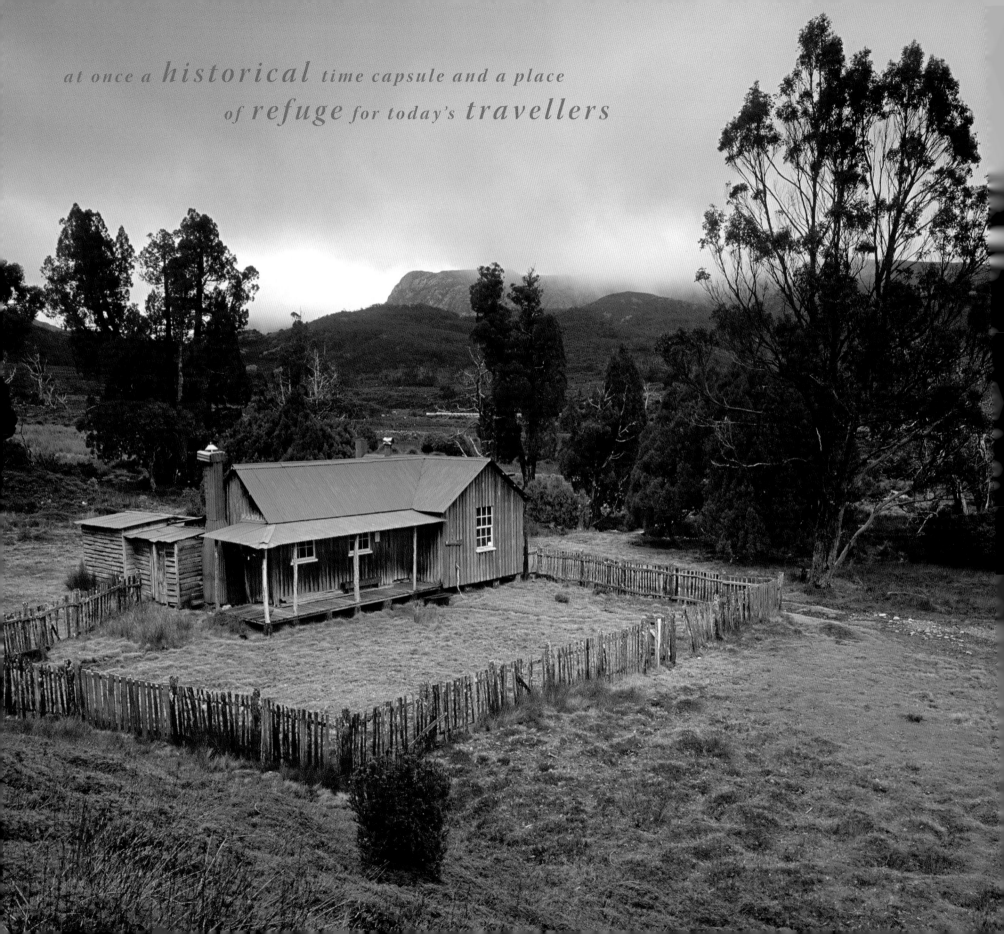

at once a *historical* time capsule and a place of *refuge* for today's *travellers*

ABOVE The old shearing shed on Muggon Station near Mullewa in Western Australia, is no longer in use.

LEFT Historic Mount Kate Hut nestles in a grassy hollow in Cradle Mountain–Lake St Clair National Park, Tasmania.

Long ago stripped of their valuable parts, these cars have been left to rust in an old car 'graveyard' in rural South Australia.

ABOVE An old petrol bowser still stands tall outside this garage in Blackall, Queensland.

RIGHT Constructed in 1889 of snow-gum slabs and sheets of iron, Wallaces Hut is the oldest mountain hut still standing on the Bogong High Plains, in Alpine National Park, Victoria.

views across the roof of the world, which seem to stretch forever

Craigs Hut, in the Victorian High Country, was built as a prop for the movie *The Man From Snowy River* (1982).

TOP The ruins of the Old Royal Hotel in Birdsville, Queensland, are listed with the National Trust.

ABOVE The old Cordillo Downs woolshed, in northern South Australia, is built of stone and tin.

RIGHT An abandoned stone homestead nestles in wheat fields near Burra, South Australia.

A rustic old hut stands isolated in rolling green fields near Killarney, Queensland.

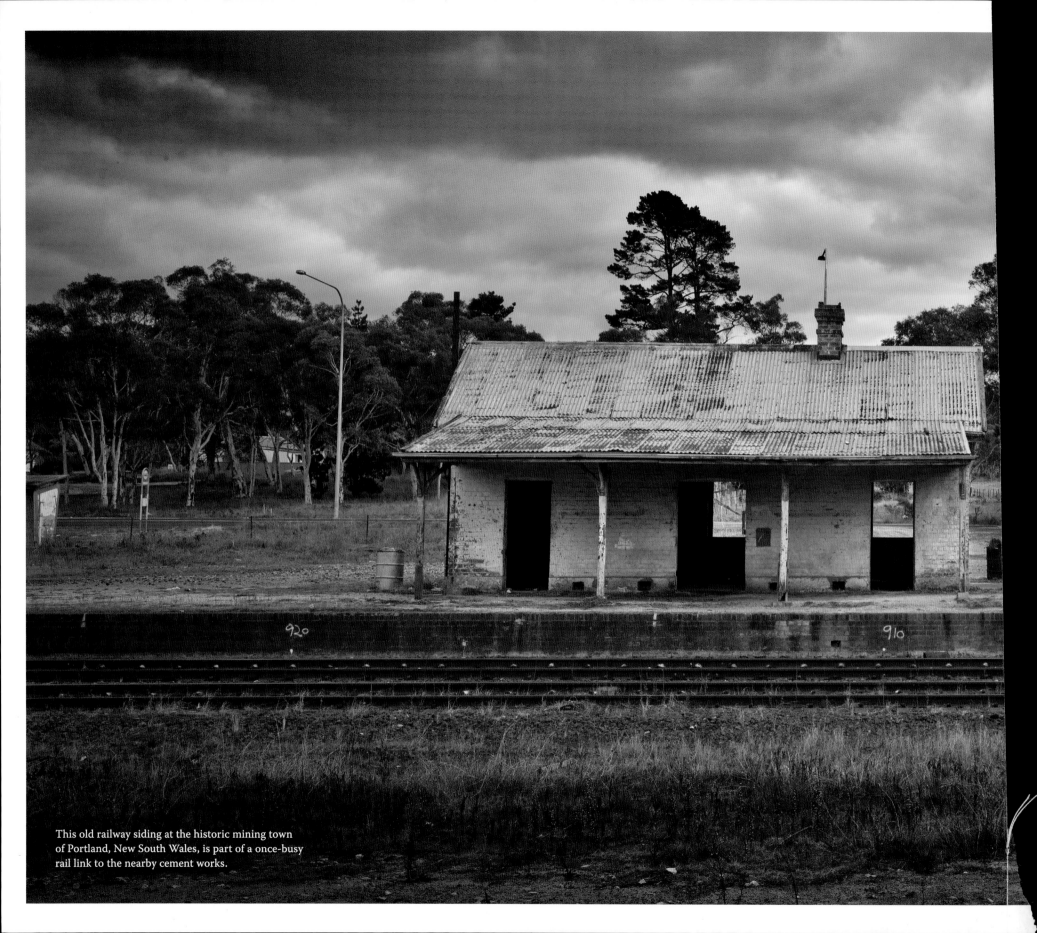

This old railway siding at the historic mining town of Portland, New South Wales, is part of a once-busy rail link to the nearby cement works.

Grey clouds roll over the lonely ruin of a stone
farm hut near Hawker, South Australia.

Sun lights up the flanks of massive grain silos at Bremer Bay, Western Australia.

BREMER BAY
EARTHMOVING
*LIMESTONE *SAND
*GRAVEL *MULCHING
*GENERAL EARTHWORKS
Colin & Corinne Hobbs

PRESENT

FOR all of its natural wonders, Australia is a thoroughly modern country and people have carved out careers and livelihoods not only in the cities but also in the most remote parts of the outback. Regardless of the climate – wet, cold, dry or hot – life goes on in these places and it's not at all unusual to find state-of-the-art businesses operating in far-flung corners of this vast continent. Huge cattle stations are run with modern efficiency, colossal mines exist where the temperatures soar to over 50°C, and much of the south-east is occupied by agricultural operations that utilise the latest techniques and equipment.

The image of the train opposite is a good example of modern businesses operating in remote regions. This is the main line into Tom Price from Karratha on the coast, and these stupendous trains operate 24/7, running uphill empty and then back down the grade full of iron ore. This particular train took a good 10 minutes to pass and I counted 244 carriages. I'm told that one train holds enough ore to make 50,000 cars.

An impossibly long Hamersley iron-ore train, having deposited its load, snakes back to the mines through the Pilbara, Western Australia.

A tiny island of scrub sits amid a sea of grain stubble in the Stirling Range, Western Australia.

the work *might be* hard, *but the* pace
of life *can still be* slow

ABOVE Visitors to an all-day rodeo enjoy refreshments, in Murgon, Queensland.

LEFT Emus forage on a tea-tree plantation near Casino, New South Wales.

Fields of golden canola create a spectacular sight on a wet, stormy day, near the Stirling Range, Western Australia.

A youngster gets in some practice before the Blinman Gymkhana, South Australia.

Viewed from a balloon, mist rises from a snaking creek in the Byron Bay hinterland, northern New South Wales.

Harvesting grain fields forms striking, uniform
patterns, near Bremer Bay, Western Australia.

finding ways
to *harvest* nature's
bounty, *sustainably*

Wind turbines line coastal cliff-tops west of Albany, Western Australia.

Viewed from above in morning light, orchard trees form neat rows near Byron Bay, New South Wales.

Towering grain silos at the port of Albany, Western Australia, await the delivery of the next harvest.

experiment and experience allow humans to slowly shape the landscape

ABOVE A station hand musters cattle at Home Valley Station in the Kimberley, Western Australia.

LEFT Forestry plantations surround native bushland in the Sunshine Coast hinterland, Queensland.

Early-morning mist cloaks lush farmland near Bridgetown, Western Australia.

A windmill rises above a fog haze, near Boulia, Queensland.

REMOTE

WHEN a country has a population of around 22 million in an area not much smaller than the mainland United States, then there are bound to be large tracts of land where very few people live. Australia's outback is renowned for its harsh conditions and, although the climate can be unforgiving, there is much beauty to be found in those wide-open spaces, where you can be the only human for hundreds of kilometres.

One of the most remote places I have ever been to is Spider Gorge, on Mornington Station in the heart of the Kimberley (p. 140). It's not accessible by road, only by helicopter – or on foot, if you know where it is. I was fortunate to be photographing the activities of the research staff in this area, and we set down here for a swim and a bite to eat while doing some aerial surveying work. It's so remote that I can't even find it on a map!

two **wheel-tracks** *through an* **endless** *plain:* **welcome** *to Central Australia*

Outback Western Australia's major east–west road link, the Gunbarrel Highway, seen here near Warburton, is most definitely for 4WDs only.

How could anyone resist a dip here? A remote, pristine waterhole, Spider Gorge is on Mornington Station, in the Kimberley, Western Australia.

Early-morning sun lights up an expanse of grassy Spinifex tufts in front of the Cockburn Ranges, Kimberley, Western Australia.

The White Stacks, eroded sandstone columns in Kennedy Range National Park, Western Australia, glow in the last light of the day.

A rocky four-wheel-drive track along the George River leads to this permanent waterhole in Millstream–Chichester National Park, in the Kimberley, Western Australia.

Crossing the flooded Pentecost River, beneath the Cockburn Range in the Kimberley, Western Australia, requires high clearance and a steady nerve.

towering ramparts mark
the ***boundaries*** *of*
an ***untamed*** *realm*

clear water, clear skies:
away from the cities,
all is *untarnished*

ABOVE A hiker enjoys a dip at Northern Rockhole, along the Jatbula Trail, in Nitmiluk National Park, Northern Territory.

RIGHT Remote places like Karijini National Park provide an opportunity to enjoy a breathtaking night sky unobscured by city lights.

The main rock-art galleries on Mount Borradaile, in the Northern Territory, are adorned with vivid, well-preserved Indigenous Australian artworks.

ABOVE Rocks in Kennedy Range National Park glow like embers in the pre-dawn light.

RIGHT Sunlight colours a dawn sky at Lorna Glen Station, north-east of Wiluna, Western Australia.

ancient outback lands
endure the endless
sculpting of wind and rain

A distant evening rain shower dampens
the dry plains at the Breakaways, near
Coober Pedy, South Australia.

Camp by Cooper Creek, Innamincka, South Australia, on a bright moonlit night, and you can sit and count the shooting stars.

This outhouse on the outskirts of Marree, South Australia, is a lone little building on a usually hot, dry plain.

COMMUNITY

Locals and visitors enjoy the annual gymkhana at Blinman, South Australia.

AUSTRALIA has a well-earned reputation as a land of practical folk, people who take some of the wilder aspects of the continent's weather in their stride and just get on with the job in hand. Nowhere is this national character more clearly revealed than in the country, especially in the outback, where life is no picnic and a considerable amount of resilience is essential.

I was commissioned by the South Australian Government to shoot a series of images on the subject of 'community'. I travelled from the north-eastern border with Queensland right across the state to almost the far south-western border with Western Australia. We had some adventures along the way and met some delightful people, and nowhere more so than in Andamooka (pp. 163–5).

Small mining communities can seem a bit uninviting when one arrives as a total stranger. But after heading into the main watering hole at Andamooka, Steve's Tuckerbox, I found that my host was also an opal miner, and it was his birthday too. Many toasts later, we were best mates, and this led to me being introduced to all the right people in town. From there on, it was easy.

Peter, an opal miner, celebrates his birthday with friends at Steve's Tuckabox Hotel in Andamooka, South Australia.

Stormy skies brood over Andamooka, South Australia, where the landscape is dotted with opal-mining spoil heaps.

ABOVE Primary-school children rehearse for their annual Strawberry Fête at Penong, South Australia.

OPPOSITE The intricate patterns of harvested grain are revealed from the air near the Stirling Range, Western Australia.

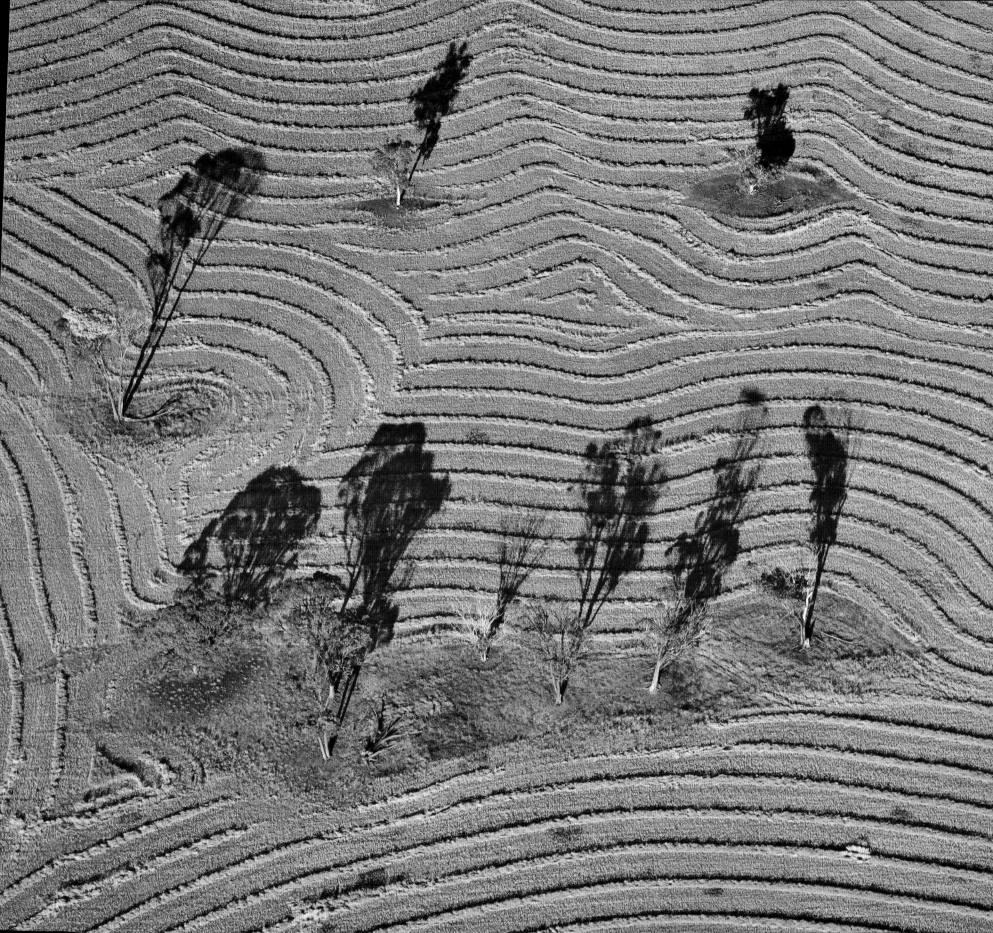

inhabitants of this *open* realm *witness*
nature's workings on a *grand* scale

Trucks like these connect communities nationwide, come rain, hail – as here, on the road near Boonah, Queensland – or shine.

Fun sculptures greet you at the visitor centre at Stonehenge, in central Queensland.

Having been mustered into a new yard, cattle settle to feeding,
at Carlton Hill Station, near Kununurra, Western Australia.

ABOVE Perched on a fence, local children enjoy the Murgon Show in Queensland.

RIGHT Rodeo riders wait for their turn in the ring at the Murgon Show, Queensland.

Red dust flies as riders drive their horses towards the finish line, in the Bracelet Race at the Blinman Gymkhana, South Australia.

in this **arduous** *land,*
competition is **keen** *and*
victories are **almost** *always*
hard *won*

ABOVE Charming murals adorn the old post office at Jundah in central Queensland.

LEFT Work starts early in the vineyards at Bellbird Heights in the Hunter Valley, New South Wales.

With the day just beginning, the main street in Katanning, Western Australia, is still deserted.

Stars illuminate a typically clear night sky above the Prairie Hotel, Parachilna, South Australia.

ACKNOWLEDGEMENTS

The publisher would like to acknowledge the following individuals and organisations:

Editorial manager
Melissa Kayser

Project manager
Lauren Whybrow

Editor
Scott Forbes

Internal page design
Peter Dyson at desertpony

Cover design
Phillip Campbell

Pre-press
Splitting Image

Explore Australia Publishing Pty Ltd
Ground Floor, Building 1, 658 Church Street,
Richmond, VIC 3121

Explore Australia Publishing Pty Ltd is a division of Hardie Grant Publishing Pty Ltd

Published by Explore Australia Publishing Pty Ltd, 2015

Form and design © Explore Australia Publishing Pty Ltd, 2015
Text and images © Nick Rains, 2015

A Cataloguing-in-Publication entry is available from the catalogue of the National Library of Australia at www.nla.gov.au

ISBN-13 9781741174878

10   9   8   7   6   5   4   3   2   1

Printed and bound in China by 1010 Printing International Ltd

Publisher's note: Every effort has been made to ensure that the information in this book is accurate at the time of going to press. The publisher welcomes information and suggestions for correction or improvement. Email: info@exploreaustralia.net.au

Publisher's disclaimer: The publisher cannot accept responsibility for any errors or omissions. The publisher cannot be held responsible for any injury, loss or damage incurred during travel. It is vital to research any proposed trip thoroughly and seek the advice of relevant state and travel organisations before you leave.

www.exploreaustralia.net.au
Find us on Facebook: www.facebook.com/exploreaustralia